AN A+B=C OF
CAMBRIDGE PROFESSORS

OPHELIA REDPATH

A Cambridge Professor is a natural phenomenon. . . .

. . . . But to define one is to get it wrong at the outset. A group of professors will never be a group; rather, a stunning collection of species.

At first glance, Cambridge professors appear to inhabit a formal garden of ideas, their personalities planted neatly within this or that row of character traits. Of course institutions have been set up to hothouse, feed and water them, with brave attempts to keep them from the harsh undergrowth of life. But at base, they are as wild as the hinterlands of New Guinea. And universities are simply their canopy.

Observe those who climb doggedly upwards, predictably straight, towards the golden glow of a Nobel, suddenly dropping dead when their quest is over. Or others, who send tendrils of enquiry into the deep shadows of history, preferring to lodge somewhere Triassic. Maybe you are familiar with the pot-plant, seemingly infertile, occupying the corner of a library for years. Just when she's all dried up and ready for compost, she'll surprise us all with a seminal explosion, spawning a movement changing the course of science forever. Some open their blooms to the wide skies of the future. Others root for every pre-digested subterranean organism in sight. There will be cross-pollinators, self-seeders, masters of camouflage and dazzle; there will be the stalwart giants of the jungle, the wilters, the virile, the prehistoric, the hybrids, the mutations and the highly specialised. Some struggle for the limelight. Most compete for a nano-space in a dusty cranny.

Whichever way they go, they, like us, are Wildlife. And there's nothing we or they can do about it.

This **ABC** is my temporary refuge from this wider fact. But I hope that within its constraints you will find personalities to enjoy and to imagine.

I dedicate these pages to my father, Theo Redpath. He was cleverer, more colourful, far lovelier than all twenty-six put together, and gave me a sense of humour to cope with being so much more ordinary.

Special thanks, Arabella, for her microscopic expertise, to Peter for his time and skill, and to my mother for making it possible for me to produce this book.

This Cambridge Professor is ...

Absurdly Accomplished

This Cambridge Professor is ...

Beginning a Book

This Cambridge Professor is ...

Contemplating Clusters

This Cambridge Professor is ...

Descended from Darwin

This Cambridge Professor is ...

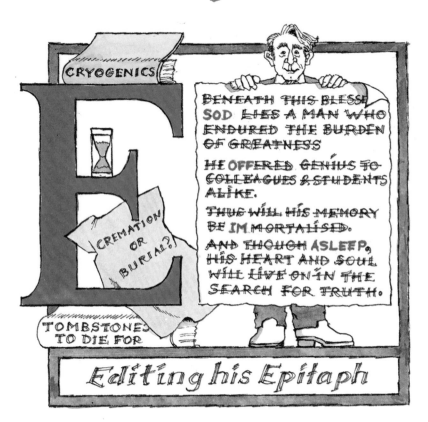

Editing his Epitaph

This Cambridge Professor is ...

Funny about Freud

This Cambridge Professor is ...

This Cambridge Professor is ...

Handwashing his Halo

This Cambridge Professor is ...

Inside

This Cambridge Professor is ...

Jurassic

This Cambridge Professor is ...

Keen on Kepler

This Cambridge Professor is ...

Laminating Leonardo

This Cambridge Professor is ...

Meddling in Moscow

This Cambridge Professor is …

Nearing a Nobel

This Cambridge Professor is ...

Obsessed with Oxford

This Cambridge Professor is ...

Pollarding Privet

This Cambridge Professor is ...

Quotable

This Cambridge Professor is ...

Reviving Rossetti

This Cambridge Professor is ...

Someone's Sophocles

This Cambridge Professor is ...

Thus, Thereby & Theretofore

This Cambridge Professor is ...

Uneasy about Utopia

This Cambridge Professor is …

Visiting Virgil

This Cambridge Professor is ...

Weird at Weekends

This Cambridge Professor is …

in Xanadu

This Cambridge Professor is ...

S bade me take life easy
as the grass grows on the weirs;
But I was young and foolish
and now am full of tears.

Down by the Salley Gardens

Yielding to Yeats

This Cambridge Professor is ...

Zonked

Theo Redpath 1913-97

Theo was born in Streatham, the only child of an engineer who co-designed the first Blue Train and Golden Arrow. He studied English at St Catherine's, Cambridge, before switching to St John's to study Philosophy. At that time he sat in at the lectures of Wittgenstein. In 1950 he was appointed first Teaching Fellow in English at Trinity and was Tutor there throughout the 60s and 70s. He held the post of University Lecturer until 1980. He loved Bach, playing bowls and exploring the vineyards of Europe. Despite being witnessed boiling a frankfurter in a kettle, he could read in 7 languages and remembered all his students' names and qualities. He is survived by his wife and three children, and though he never met his eight grandchildren, they will grow to know him. As we speak, a Theo-shaped gap is gradually being filled for them with tales of their unforgettable grandfather.

THE AUTHOR

Ophelia was born in Cambridge in 1965. Her mother, a musician, her father, an English don at Trinity College, Cambridge, and her grandparents, both artists, all gave her plenty to think about.

She has since followed a career as a painter, exhibiting both in Britain and abroad. She also works graphically, and is designing prints and books, focusing on thinkers, historical periods, wildlife, musicians, artists, and other passions. She will be thus employed until her eyesight deteriorates.

She currently lives outside Cambridge in a cottage by a field with her daughter, Sally, two cats and four fish.

First published in the United Kingdom in 2016 by:
PANGOLIN POST,
2 River Farm Cottages, 2 Harston Road,
Haslingfield, Cambridge CB23 1JX

Designed by Ophelia Redpath and Peter Mennim
Printed & bound in Great Britain by:
W G Baird
Greystone Press, Caulside Drive,
Antrim BT41 2RS

This copy is from the first print-run of the first Edition.
www.opheliaredpath.co.uk
Email: opheliaredpath@btinternet.com

ISBN 978-0-9954943-0-5